Bouquets

a year of flowers & settings for the table

Marsha Heckman

Photographs by Jay Graham

welcome
BOOKS

NEW YORK & SAN FRANCISCO

Published in 2005 by Welcome Books®
An imprint of Welcome Enterprises, Inc.
6 West 18th Street, New York, NY 10011
(212) 989-3200; Fax (212) 989-3205
www.welcomebooks.com

Publisher: Lena Tabori
Project Director: Natasha Tabori Fried
Designer: Gregory Wakabayashi
Editorial Assistant: Bethany Cassin Beckerlegge

Distributed to the trade in the U.S. and Canada by
Andrews McMeel Distribution Services
U.S. Order Department and Customer Service
Toll-free: (800) 943-9839; Orders-only Fax: (800) 943-9831
PUBNET S&S San Number: 200-2442
Canada Toll-free: (888) 268-3216; Orders-only Fax: (888) 849-8151

Design and compilation copyright © 2005 Welcome Enterprises, Inc.
Text copyright © 2005 Marsha Heckman
Photographs copyright © 2005 Jay Graham

Library of Congress Cataloging-in-Publication Data on file

ISBN 1-932183-25-6

Printed in China

10 9 8 7 6 5 4 3 2 1

contents

introduction

I was the daughter who set the table in our house. I loved arranging the flowers and bringing out the "good dishes" and linens from the china cabinet and the kitchen cupboards to make pretty settings for dinner. From age ten I was encouraged to help with family parties and my aunt's "lady lunches." I got lavish praise from the grown-ups.

My mother and grandmother always made special decorations for every holiday: paper-and-doily Valentines, shamrock cutouts for Saint Patrick's Day, elaborately colored Easter eggs, and woven paper baskets filled with flowers from our garden (and, I confess, the neighbors' gardens) for May Day. For Halloween we cut out skeleton garlands and carved pumpkins with scary faces lit by candles inside. Thanksgiving and Christmas brought out the decorations, the best china and, of course, flowers to arrange complementing the holiday theme. For special occasions, my mom shares the dishes she has inherited and collected for many years, so my sisters and I have continued our family custom to this day.

The inspiration for this book came to me when my mother and I went on a trip to Hong Kong and Indonesia. Time-zone changes left us unable to sleep, so we lay in our beds and invented fantasy table settings with ideas for pretty flower arrangements until we nodded off. I thought sharing how we used our own and borrowed items to create entertaining tables would be fun and inspire readers to set tables that invite compliments and start conversations. We all are entertaining at home more than ever today, and a table set with care and imagination makes your guests feel especially welcome. More couples are opting to have their weddings at home too, renting the furniture and tableware and making the flower arrangements themselves.

Setting the table is like dressing for a party. You take your theme from the event or from your favorite flowers, dishes, or linens. Dress the table with the cloth and complimentary china in matching or contrasting colors. Add napkins as you would a belt or scarf, and finish with the jewelry—

shiny flatware, napkin rings, candles, and place cards or favors. Your centerpiece is the fabulous hat or corsage that sets off your outfit for the occasion.

This book gives you ideas for making your table beautiful, creating an atmosphere that makes your guests and family feel special. I encourage you to bring out your wedding china and family treasures from the cupboard, look for bargains to embellish the table, and try dramatic color combinations, fun accessories, and easy-to-create centerpieces with flowers from every season of the year.

The centerpiece is the star of the table. Using simple techniques and a few basic tools and supplies, you can make a wonderful flower arrangement. Be imaginative about the containers—serving pieces, boxes, buckets, a fish bowl, seashells, or a teapot work as well as a vase or basket. Mirror the design on your china with the same flowers or colors for a coordinated look.

A gorgeous table doesn't have to be set with fancy or expensive items. And the dishes don't have to match. You can mix plain dinner plates with salad plates and cups of a different pattern and add a collection of mismatched glasses and silverware. Charity shops, garage sales, flea markets, and discount and import stores are great sources for inexpensive flower containers, flatware, glasses, and linens. Make sure to check out the resource guide in the back of this book to help you find most of the items I've used on the tables. Some were generously loaned to me for this book, some were purchased in national chain stores, and some can be found online.

If you don't have the perfect tablecloth, use a sheet, fabric, or a curtain panel. White linens are not the most exciting, so bring on color, and contrast the napkins with the tablecloth. Try dyeing plain white napkins to complement your dishes. I've dyed the same cotton napkins several times. I just soak them in bleach between uses and dye them again. You can make place cards on your computer— use any font you wish and print them on cardstock or glossy photo paper. Or decorate the table with souvenirs from your travels, your precious collections, and even your old costume jewelry.

When you have a large party, borrow from your family and friends. My rule is you must invite the person who loans you their tableware. The spring wedding in this book has several tables. Each one is different, decorated with possessions of the couple's sisters or friends.

Preparation to entertain at home can be as much fun as the party itself, and the reward for your effort is so satisfying for both you and your guests. They will appreciate all the thought and planning you put into creating warmth and drama on a well-decorated table, and will respond by having a great time.

spring

Entertaining in springtime gives you opportunities to beautify the table with flowering branches, tulips and callas, crocus and daffodils, or hyacinth and lilies of the valley. Afternoon tea or a girls' lunch are wonderful occasions to bring out your best silver and china and share those treasures hidden in your closet. Friends and family can come together to create individual table settings with easy-to-make spring bouquet centerpieces for a wedding in your own garden. Children can contribute their artistic talents to a Mother's Day breakfast they put together themselves—with a little help from Grandma or Dad.

birds:
a spring celebration

Eggs are a symbol of new beginnings in every culture in the world. Whether you celebrate Easter or Passover in the spring, the egg has a simple beauty and significance that can add charm to your table. Pair them in a centerpiece with the most beautiful flowers of the season—branches of creamy dogwood blossoms, graceful and fragrant lilacs, and tiny flowers from spring bulbs. This elegant table celebrates spring with soft greens, sky blues, and dishes with beautiful drawings of birds transferred onto each one. Any tableware in the soft pastel shades of springtime will make a lovely party table, or combine white plates with linens in spring colors for your celebration.

The hand-painted mirror-backed glass place cards (above) from the 1930s were a birthday gift from my dear friend Sunshine. After the party, you can erase the name on the frosted-glass panel and use them for another celebration.

The spring centerpiece (right) is a Victorian wire basket lined with angel vine that has been formed into the shape of bird nests. Eggshells, each holding a bouquet of tiny bulb flowers, fill the basket, and dogwood branches with pale-green blossoms sit in the center. The branches are tall, but do not obstruct the guests' view of each other.

birds basket how-to

For this very large table I made 10 nests and 12 eggs.

Small liner or low-sided vase
Low basket
Florist clay
Floral pin frog
3-4 Dogwood branches
Angel vine (also called mattress vine)
Eggs
Grape hyacinth (Muscari)
Miniature daffodils
Allium
Lily of the valley
Forget-me-nots
Green sticky tape
Reindeer moss
Rubber bands

Place a low vase or plastic liner that is about one-third the size of the basket and secure it with a piece of florist clay on the bottom center of the basket.

Attach a floral pin frog inside the liner with clay.

Smash the bottom two inches of the dogwood branches so they can absorb water.

Anchor the dogwood branches well into the pin frog.

Add water after you put the arrangement on the table to avoid spilling.

Coil several strands of angel vine and twist into a circle, winding the ends together to make a nest shape. Repeat.

Fill the basket with "nests," covering the liner and frog.

The centerpiece eggs are filled with (below, top to bottom) grape hyacinth (Muscari), miniature daffodils, alliums, lily of the valley, and forget-me-nots.

Crack the egg about one-third down from the pointed end by rapping it sharply with a knife.

Gently remove the top and empty the eggshell. (I usually make eggs Benedict for Easter breakfast with the yolks and save the whites for cake frosting or meringue shells for dessert.)

Wash the shell.

Cut the stems of your flowers to about three to four inches and make little bunches of three to six flowers each.

Fasten the stems together at the bottom with sticky green tape.

Wrap the stems in some wet reindeer moss and secure with a rubber band.

Place the flowers and moss inside the larger piece of eggshell.

Arrange the eggs in the angel vine nests in the basket.

lilac arrangement how-to

The sideboard displays the bird-pattern serving pieces flanked by two generous bouquets of white lilacs in muted green Victorian wire baskets.

10 Branches of lilacs cut to 12- to 24-inch lengths.

⮞ Smash the bottom two inches to expose the woody stems inside the bark so that they can absorb water.

⮞ Place wet floral foam cut to size inside a six-inch flowerpot without a drain hole. Arrange the shorter stems around the edge of the container.

⮞ Place the longest stems in the center, then fill in with the remaining lilacs to form a dome-shaped bouquet.

⮞ Put the pot inside the baskets to finish.

afternoon tea

A tea party is a great way to host a wedding

or baby shower or to introduce visitors to your friends at an afternoon gathering. Serve tiny sandwiches and desserts passed to your guests on trays and set up a table with a variety of teas for the guests to choose their favorite brew. I rely on borrowing from my friends when I entertain and need more dishes to accommodate a crowd. My rule is that the person who loans me tableware is always invited to the party.

When you mix different styles of dishes on the same table, group them separately, and use linens and flowers that complement every pattern's color palette. For this table (opposite) I use a pale-yellow cloth divided into three sections by a flowered yellow ribbon. Three varieties of yellow spring-bulb flowers decorate the center.

I tie one daffodil at the table's edge (left) and secure it with a straight pin underneath the cloth.

This tea was held at my friend Ruth's beautiful house in early spring. She owns the unusual china teapot and cups with handles made to look like branch coral (left). We use them to serve green tea with candied ginger and sweet Meyer lemon. I made the little stirrers from seashells to complement the ceramic coral.

The flowered-china teapot and vintage china cups (opposite left) belong to my mother. These cups—each one a different design—used to be called "engagement cups." In the first half of the twentieth century, it was customary for women to give a teacup to a prospective bride to celebrate her engagement and start a collection of her own dishes. The antique spoons were the collection of

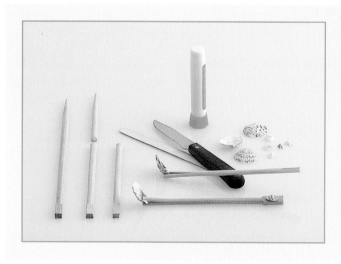

seashell stirrer how-to

Bamboo chopstick
Small round seashell (approx. three-quarters-inch diameter)
Super glue
Tiny seashell

🐚 Cut the chopstick six inches from the thick end.
🐚 With a paring knife carefully split the cut end.
🐚 Put a dot of glue on the front and back of the flat side of the seashell and insert it into the split. Hold the shell in place while the glue sets.
🐚 Decorate the handle with a small shell or bit of coral.

my Great-Uncle Henry. The vintage napkins are each different and were found at antique fairs and flea markets. Old linen and cotton can be revived by soaking in a strong mixture of warm water and an enzyme whitener. Rinse them thoroughly and iron while slightly damp.

The pastel ceramic tea set (above right) is my own. It is a new version of the Art Deco Fiesta tableware designed by Fredrick Hurton Rhead that was manufactured from 1936 until it was discontinued in 1973. Reissued in 1986 in new colors, Fiestaware is affordable and available in department stores today. The tea napkins were embellished with a crocheted edge and embroidered by my grandmother in the 1940s.

Spring makes its debut with the appearance of bright bulb flowers—crocuses, tulips, hyacinths, and daffodils. Bouquets of their yellow blooms are a cheerful centerpiece for any spring table. In the Victorian flower language, the message of the yellow tulip is "I'm hopelessly in love with you," and the hyacinth tells the loved one "I want to play with you." Daffodils, which represent joy, chivalry, and devotion, say to the receiver "you have a sweet disposition." Ironically, daffodils are poisonous. Never mix daffodils with other flowers in a vase—the alkaloids in the daffodil's sap will kill them.

centerpiece how-to

The flowers are arranged in a traditional silver teapot, creamer, and sugar bowl (opposite). A ceramic tea set like this (above) gives a more casual look.

5 *Yellow hyacinth*
24 *Daffodils*
24 *Tulips*
3 *Rubber bands*

❧ Each bouquet is made in the hand by adding flowers one at a time in a spiral pattern to create a dome shape.
❧ Adjust the flowers and secure the stems with a rubber band as close to the blooms as possible.
❧ Cut the stems with a knife one inch shorter than the depth of your container. Using a knife rather than scissors prevents crushing the stems—which will inhibit their ability to draw water.

rose:
a pink table

Your grandmother's "good dishes" are most likely hidden in a closet or gathering dust in your mother's china cabinet. Bring them out and enjoy the beautiful plates and cups, for they were meant to be used. Most antique china has a floral pattern. Try replicating the design in your centerpiece by using the same flowers and color palette. It will enhance the fine qualities of old tableware. Match the napkins to the strongest color on the dishes rather than old-fashioned plain white linens. And for a more contemporary look, show off the wood of your table instead of using a tablecloth. Small flowers will make fresh and pretty napkin rings, and your guests can wear them as wrist corsages.

Every once in awhile I invite my girlfriends for an old-fashioned ladies' lunch, and borrow the beautiful china my mom inherited from Great-Great Aunt Elsie, who crated and shipped her French Limoge wedding dishes to Havana, Cuba,

where she lived at the American Embassy in the early 1900s.

My friend, Barbara, hosted this luncheon in her French–inspired, pink dining room. Barbara's blush-colored etched-crystal glasses and sterling silverware complement the rose garland pattern of the fine china perfectly. The feminine formality of the *rose* table evokes genteel behavior and memories of a more gracious time for gentle ladies.

We all felt we should be wearing hats and gloves.

The tabletop garden of small potted plants, a Myrtle topiary, and some lilies of the valley sits on an oval-shaped plastic tray. We put an antique Limoge shepherdess with her kneeling lover in the garden on our French table. But you could add a porcelain doll, animal figurines, or a miniature garden bench to complete the fantasy scene for yours.

flower napkin ring how-to

Each fresh flower napkin ring is made with the following:

10-inch piece of cloth-covered #22 florist wire
16 inches of one-quarter–inch-wide ribbon
One or two stems of pink wax flower
Florist's tape

🪸 Make a small loop at each end of the wire and twist to close.

🪸 Tie an eight-inch piece of ribbon to each end above the loop.

🪸 Clip 10 or 12 flower clusters from the wax flower stems.

🪸 Place a cluster of flowers on the wire, covering the loop.

🪸 Secure the stems with floral tape. Pull the tape as you wind it around the stem and wire—the tape sticks to itself when stretched.

🪸 Continue adding flowers on top of the tape until you have covered the wire.

🪸 Bend the napkin ring into an oval shape and tie it on the napkin at the back.

centerpiece how-to

The miniature garden includes plants that can be found at any nursery.

A flat of Scotch moss, creeping fig, myrtle topiary, maidenhair fern, and Neanthe Bella parlor palm (back row, left to right) 10 stems of lily of the valley (each in a small spiked water tube), African violet, and miniature rose (front row, left to right). Lily of the valley is available in pots at the nursery in the spring, or the imported cut flowers can be ordered from the florist.

🪸 Cut the moss into three-inch-wide strips and take away some of the soil on one side. Fit the strips of moss around the edge of the container (overlapping the side where you have removed some soil) to cover the edge.

🪸 Remove the plants from their pots and arrange them in the tray.

🪸 Tuck the plants in next to the moss, and then fill in the middle of the garden with the remaining moss.

🪸 Cut the stems of the lily of the valley to two to three inches and fit each one with a small leaf into the pointed water tubes.

🪸 Place them in the garden, making sure to hide the rubber top of the tube in the moss.

🪸 Mist the garden with water every day and it will last for weeks, except the lily of the valley, which will last only a few days.

mother's day
&
father's day

Children should learn to set the table properly

when they are very young. It is one of the few matters of etiquette left to pass down today, and ought to be practiced often as part of the important family ritual of sitting down to eat together. In my family, it is a tradition for the kids to make breakfast for Mom on Mother's Day, and in the summer for Dad on Father's Day. A simple container filled with flowers the kids can pick in your own garden is the cheerful centerpiece. A plate for French toast or a bowl for cereal with a juice glass and cup for coffee or tea is all that is needed. It's very easy for young children to set a breakfast table in the garden or the kitchen.

These adorable plates (opposite) were hand painted by nine-year-old Samantha Stevens when her grandmother took her to a "paint your own" ceramics studio. These studios are everywhere and are a fun and creative activity for families. You paint your own design on the ceramic and leave it to be fired in the studio kiln. Samantha and her little brother, Ryan, personalized the plain square of canvas with their handprints for the tablecloth. We used fabric paint from the craft store. Simply spread a thin layer of paint in a pie tin, press the hand into the paint, and then press it onto the cloth. Follow directions on the paint label to treat the fabric.

To create the centerpiece, 15 to 20 Icelandic poppies in sunny shades of yellow, coral, and orange are placed in a glass milk bottle (above). You can use an old bottle or acquire a new one by purchasing a quart of organic milk at the health food store.

"share the

wealth" wedding

A different friend of the bride dressed each table at this reception. Often, family and close friends are anxious to contribute and participate in a wedding or special occasion celebration. One meaningful way to involve the generosity and creativity of loved ones is to ask them to do one table with their own dishes and to make a centerpiece complementing their setting. Here, the bride unified the look with matching tables and chairs and green under cloths to fit the garden location of the event. Flowers are different on each table, but they are all white.

Each table will be different and give the bride's friends the chance to be designers. Lena made a retro-thirties table with her California pottery,

Depression glass, and a vase from her wonderful collection of McCoy pottery. Sarah did an Asian theme based on the bamboo pattern of her dishes. Cathy expressed her love of Art Deco with calla lilies. I used my favorite tablecloth and dishes with the ivy design. Claudia brought elegant china and linens together with spectacular peonies.

Lena sets a 1930's-style table (above) with lush colors of Bauer pottery plates and pink Depression glass. The linens, which were her grandmother's, are a soft green damask. A white McCoy vase holds the bouquet of twenty creamy French tulips with their stems cut to the height of the vase, and a tiny tulip graces each guest's place.

Sarah mixed her 1950's Noritake "Orient"-pattern china, which she inherited from her grandmother, with napkin rings and flatware that perfectly echo the bamboo design painted on the dishes. She added contemporary natural woven place mats, parchment napkins, and glasses. The orchid centerpiece—six stems of phalaenopsis orchids surrounded by ten stems of dendrobium orchids in a square of floral foam within a plastic liner—is arranged in a handmade bamboo box, which finishes the Asian theme of the table.

My table is set with the Franciscan "Ivy" dishes I have collected for years. The glasses have etched grapes and leaves, which dress up the earthenware beautifully. I decorated the napkins with an ivy leaf glued to a simple wired ribbon. My branch flatware mimics the ivy stems on the dishes.

Two dozen garden roses in a vase are placed in the center of an earthenware urn surrounded by four ivy plants.

Cathy decorated her Art Deco-inspired table with a plain round glass bowl brimming with 24 calla lilies from her garden. They are arranged by crisscrossing the stems, with one calla lily under the water. To the inexpensive china painted with calla lilies and a black-and-silver striped rim, she adds a matte-silver charger, a simple yellow tablecloth, and napkins embellished with real miniature calla lilies. Her modern stainless flatware and the swirled champagne flutes are new.

Claudia used white cutwork linens by Lenox and beautiful fine china. A gorgeous display of 20 peonies placed close together in a tooled-metal box from India with jeweled handles fills the middle of her table. Claudia chose flatware and crystal with a gold rim to match her dishes.

The simple cake (opposite) is topped with a bisque bride and groom and sprinkled with rose petals. Roses are edible if they are washed and have been grown without spray of any kind. The pink Depression–glass dessert dishes are from Lena's collection, and my grandmother made the pink embroidered tablecloth.

summer

Inside or outdoors summer is the time to get together with friends and family and have fun creating decor that starts conversations and makes everyone feel special from your efforts. Summer entertaining can be plain or fancy, from an elegant dinner to a Fourth of July picnic by the lake or pool. This season's flowers are bright and plentiful. You can create a gorgeous display of garden roses or make a travel-themed dinner with palm leaves and orchids, dress up a picnic with sweet peas, or create an all-white wedding with hydrangeas or summer's blooming herbs.

americana:
a holiday picnic

Red, white, and blue enamelware pots hold corn

on the cob and potato salad or baked beans for a traditional picnic with fried chicken, barbecued hamburgers, or the American picnic favorite, hot dogs. Use a couple of yards of denim fabric to cover the table or to spread out on the grass or sand. The

table is a celebration of Americana for Memorial Day, Labor Day, or Fourth of July. Add watermelon or ice cream and apple pie with cups of hot coffee to enjoy during the fireworks.

Plastic or paper plates and an enamel cup for lemonade and for coffee are right for any outdoor meal. The silverware from a discount store is almost as inexpensive as plastic, and reusable. Place it in a toy sand pail or other portable container like these tin berry buckets painted with stars and stripes. Put in a folded dishtowel as a napkin, and add boxes of sparklers for everyone.

centerpiece how-to

Simple little bunches of red, white, and blue flowers are
an easy-to-transport centerpiece for a patriotic holiday
picnic or barbecue. Keep them secure by placing them in
buckets of sand, which are the perfect containers to light
up the party with sparklers. The sand provides safety in
case of any fireworks mishaps during the celebration.

3 Four-and-a-half-inch enamel buckets
6 Cups sand
Water
10 Stems red sweet peas
10 Stems white sweet peas

10 Stems delphinium
3 Sparklers (optional)

  Add one cup of sand to each bucket. Cover the sand
with water.
  Arrange the red sweet peas in a neat bunch in your
hand.
  Put the bunch of red sweet peas into the wet sand at
an angle to one side of the bucket, burying the stems well.
  Add one cup of sand to the bucket.
  Repeat with the white sweet peas and the
delphinium in the other two buckets.
  Place one sparkler in each bucket, angling them in
the opposite direction of the flowers.

american flag how-to

For a patriotic holiday party at home why not create the American flag for your buffet or barbecue table? This one is simple to make. Two plastic box photo frames are the container. You could do a larger version, but keep the proportion the same and increase the number of flowers proportionally.

2 Blocks floral foam
2 Eight- by ten-inch plastic box photo frames
36–46 Bachelor buttons
6 Stephanotis flowers
32–40 Red roses
24–36 White roses

～ Soak the floral foam in water for two hours.
～ Cut the foam lengthwise to fit into each frame, trim the foam evenly to the height of the frame by drawing a large knife across the top surface of the frame.

～ Place the frames next to each other, 10-inch sides together.
～ Cut the stems of the bachelor buttons to about one and a half inches and stick them into the upper right of one frame forming a five-inch square. If the stems are soft, poke a hole in the foam with a skewer before placing the flower.
～ Add the stephanotis in rows into the square of bachelor buttons for the stars.
～ Cut the rose stems to one and a half inches.
～ Make rows of roses for stripes across both frames starting with red at the top, alternating red and white, ending with a red stripe.

treasure:
elegant entertaining

The accessories on your table are like the jewelry

in an ensemble you wear. These glasses and votive cups in the colors of precious stones were the inspiration for this table. Eastern flair is provided by Indian sari silk chair covers and the mirrored table covering that is actually a curtain panel. Table linen need not be a tablecloth. Be imaginative with a washable curtain, a piece of fabric, a sari cloth, or even a lightweight rug. Jeweled napkin rings are easy to make and echo the rich colors of the glasses. The candles and sumptuous garden-rose table bouquet are set on mirror tiles from the hardware store to add sparkle and magnify the candlelight.

You don't need expensive possessions to create a rich-looking table for a dinner party. The cut glass and my mother's beautiful china are luxurious, but you could use any dishes with a gold rim, or do a silver version with stainless utensils and a silver flower container for the same effect. Faux-gold flatware complements the gold detail on this china.

Garden roses are descendent of the older varieties of rose grown before 1867, when the first tea-rose hybrid was introduced. Many rose lovers prefer these older varieties because their shape is more natural and their perfume is more intense than the newer varieties. An infinite number of garden roses is available today due to the patient and productive growers who specialize in the beautiful and fragrant blooms the Greeks called "the queen of flowers."

centerpiece how-to

Three tiers of gorgeous jewel-studded garden roses in graduated sizes of containers make the centerpiece. The soft golden beige is called "Peter B," the bold yellow is "Gold Medal," the yellow with the red edge is "Perfect Moment," the small red is a very old rose named "Francois Rebelas," the larger red is "Ingrid Bergman," and the striped one is "Scentimental."

1 1/2 Blocks floral foam
Sticky green tape

1 Container with eight-inch opening
1 Container with five-inch opening
62 Garden roses (approximately)
1 Container with three-inch opening
Fake gems from the craft store
Fabric glue

❧ Soak the floral foam in water for two hours.
❧ Cut foam to fit in the largest container and secure it with the sticky tape.
❧ Cut foam to fit your middle-size container plus one inch above the sides; secure it with the sticky tape.
❧ Place the middle-size container on top of the large one.
❧ Cut the stems of roses one at a time and stick them into the foam in the bottom container so they overhang the rim by about two inches.
❧ Make two or three rows of roses, covering the foam completely.
❧ For the medium container, cut the stems of the roses one at a time to about three inches and stick them straight into the sides of the exposed foam, leaving space on the top for the small vase.
❧ Fill the small container with water and arrange the remaining roses into a tight dome shape.
❧ Attach a few fake gems to the petals of the roses in the top container with a drop of fabric glue.

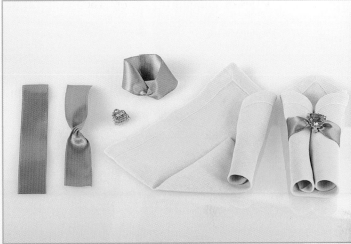

napkin how-to

Seven inches of one-and-a-half-inch-wide wired-satin ribbon
for each napkin ring

Fabric glue or matching thread

Clip-on earrings (one for each napkin ring)

◦ Twist the ribbon twice in the center.

◦ Sew or glue the ribbon ends together.

◦ Clip an old earring onto the twisted part
of the ribbon.

Napkin fold:

◦ Fold the napkin in half, and half again.

◦ Iron the napkin.

◦ Place the napkin diagonally, folded edge at the
bottom, corner points at the top.

◦ Fold the bottom point of the napkin one-third
toward the top point.

◦ Roll the sides in toward the center neatly.

◦ Slip the ring onto the center of the folded napkin.

kauai:
a tropical
experience

A fun way to personalize a dinner party table

is to use souvenirs and a centerpiece that bring back memories of a wonderful trip and share them with friends. Use a Mexican serape as a tablecloth with plain pottery dishes and paper flowers to remember your vacation in Acapulco. Lay a sari cloth on the table with brass charger plates, little carved statues, and a bouquet of yellow and magenta flowers recalling your travels in India.

At this dinner party, Aloha spirit takes the guests on a little island vacation on the deck. Everyone at

the Kauai table is given a dendrobium orchid lei welcoming them to a sunset dinner overlooking the blue Pacific Ocean. Tropical fruit punch or *piña coladas* are served in these gorgeous glasses etched with palm trees, and dinner is enjoyed on plates painted with a nostalgic tropical scene. (You could substitute any plate with a palm tree or tropical flower design.) The island atmosphere is created with fabulous Hawaiian orchids in seashells, pineapple votives, dashboard hula dolls, and an easy-to-make miniature palm tree.

Hawaiian leis can be ordered year round online. The pineapple votive holder, *wahini* candles, and hula dolls are souvenirs from Hawaii, and I made the napkins with aloha-shirt fabric. The bamboo flatware is very inexpensive, and the table covering is a woven-paper window blind together with raffia hula skirts. The palm-tree candlesticks, dinner plates, beautiful salad plates, and etched-crystal glasses enhance the tropical theme.

centerpiece how-to

The colors of the flowers—neon orange, bright yellow, vibrant magenta, purple, and green—are as spectacular as a Kauai sunset's flash over the ocean just as the sun disappears under the horizon. My grandson Julian made the palm tree.

1 ¹/2-inch wide cardboard mailing tube at least 24 inches long
Sand
1 large brown paper bag
Dark brown watercolor paint
Glue
1 4- by 4-inch block of floral foam
10 cut palm leaves
15 cattleya orchids
10 lime-green and yellow cymbidiums
Several large seashells

🪸 Cut tube to desired height and fill halfway with sand for weight.

🪸 Tear brown paper bag into strips.

🪸 Tint one edge of the paper strips with the dark brown watercolor paint.

🪸 Apply glue to one side of the strips and wrap the strips around the tube starting at the top and working down to the base.

🪸 Stick the floral foam firmly on top of the tube and arrange the palm leaves.

🪸 Tuck the cattleya and cymbidiums—all in their water tubes—inside the seashells and arrange around the base of the tree.

children's birthday party

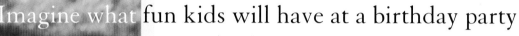

Imagine what fun kids will have at a birthday party where they can eat "bugs"! The center of this table in the park is grass and daisies with a host of adorable edible insects. Parents will appreciate the fact that the bugs and cupcakes are healthy snacks containing very little sugar. But the kids will never guess. They'll be too busy devouring delicious ladybugs and spiders, tasty butterflies, and caterpillar parts.

Bright striped paper plates, matching napkins, forks and spoons, and "crazy straws" in unbreakable plastic cups are fun, and very inexpensive. To encourage the kids to drink milk I spice it up with a recipe my own children called "Mom's magic milk." Add a few drops of vanilla, a teaspoon of raw sugar, and food coloring—a different color for each child.

Mini chocolate chips
Butter frosting (see recipe below)
Muffins
Dinner rolls
Peanut butter and/or cream cheese
Jam or jelly
Green grapes
Raisins
Peaches, nectarines, tangerines, or plums
Round melon
8 Small red bananas, or finger bananas
1 Lemon
1 Lime
Pretzels (standard size)
Cream cheese or soft American cheese (one-by-two-inch square per butterfly)
Sesame seeds

Frosting recipe

1/2 teaspoon vanilla extract
1 cube (1/2 cup) soft butter
2 cups confectioners sugar
Food coloring

🍃 Mix vanilla into butter, add sugar 1/2 cup at a time and mix well, and then use several drops food coloring for desired color.

Ladybug and snail

🍃 To create a tasty garden snail, remove the strawberry stem and slice the thick end to hold one Chinese pea pod.

centerpiece how-to

This square of wheat grass is crawling with edible bugs. Kids will be delighted by strawberry-and-pea pod snails, cheese-and-pretzel butterflies, peach spiders, caterpillar sandwiches, muffin ladybugs, and a big melon creature with mini-banana legs. Every bug is healthy food and irresistible birthday party fare.

Note: With very small children be sure to remove all toothpicks before serving.

Toothpicks
Wooden skewers
One-by-three-foot rectangle wheat grass, trimmed to two to three inches high in the center
Melon baller
Parchment or wax paper
Three-inch terra-cotta flowerpots
Birthday candles
10 daisies(for garnish)
Figure amounts of food according to number of your guests:
Strawberries
Chinese pea pods
Mini muffins

Secure the pea pod with a toothpick broken in half.

Homemade or store-bought blueberry or corn mini muffins become ladybugs when topped with red butter frosting and spotted with mini chocolate chips.

Caterpillar

The birthday caterpillar is made with round dinner rolls sliced in half and filled with kid-favorite sandwich makings: peanut butter or cream cheese with jelly and/or raisins.

His eyes are green grapes cut in half, attached with a toothpick and studded with a raisin.

His antennae are raisins on toothpicks.

A wooden skewer anchors the standing sections of his body into the wheat grass.

Spider

Toothpick legs and raisin eyes create a yummy (and healthy) spider from a peach or nectarine, or even a tangerine or plum.

Watermelon bug

The big bug is actually a small round watermelon, but any round melon will do nicely.

Cut a triangular section of the melon rind and scoop out the inside with a melon baller. Put the melon balls back inside the melon.

Cut four small holes on each side of the melon near the bottom, and stick one

end of a small red banana in each hole for legs.

The eyes are simply a slice of lemon topped with a slice of lime and half a grape. Hold them in place with a toothpick.

Serve the melon balls from the opening on top.

Butterfly

Regular-size pretzels are the wings of the butterfly, which is made by rolling a two-by-one-inch piece of soft

American cheese or cream cheese in sesame seeds.

Add two pretzel "wings" and refrigerate on a sheet of parchment or waxed paper.

Wood skewers hold the butterflies above the wheat grass lawn on the table.

Cupcakes

The colorful cupcakes in tiny flowerpots are really muffins with a little frosting and a candle in each one. They are a less messy, more nutritious version of the birthday cake.

white

summer wedding

From the linens to the favors, everything is clean

and sparkling white at this summer wedding reception. A monochromatic design is cool, elegant, and luxurious. White is the freshest look for a hot summer day. Fans are the party favors keeping the guests cool, and each guest is given a tiny bit of cake in a white box to take home. The place cards are also a fan, and the centerpieces are embellished with fans completing the summer theme.

The table is set with rentals and a pretty white tablecloth on top for a personal touch. Each table has a different cloth, some with embroidery or lace trim. The fan place cards are made with computer-printed names on plain white paper. Using the printing option of "landscape" layout so the names are formatted horizontally, type two names per sheet of paper. Choose your favorite font and put two or three spaces between the letters so that they are readable when the paper is folded. Cut the paper in half lengthwise and fold each half in three-quarter-inch sections. Use double-sided carpet tape to secure the place card to the tablecloth.

There is a great variety of choices in rentals to create a large party or wedding today. Tables in every size and shape and chairs with pretty chair covers make your look distinctive. Here, the furniture, table linens, flatware, glasses, and square white plates are all rentals.

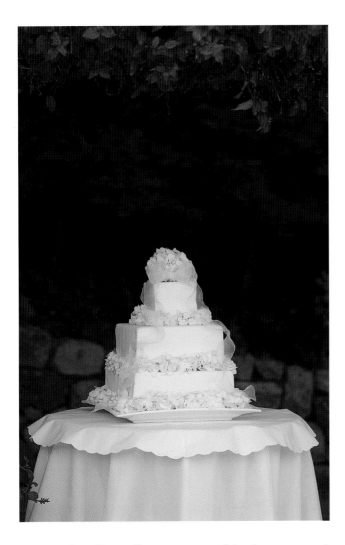

centerpiece how-to

Hydrangeas make a dramatic statement for your money and are available in shades of blue, pink, burgundy, pale green, or white. This aptly named flower needs lots of water; the blossoms absorb more water than their stems. When conditioned properly hydrangeas will last for weeks and hold up well on a hot day.

8 Large hydrangea
3 Sheets heavy paper
6 Wooden skewers
White adhesive tape

Fill the kitchen sink or tub with cool water. Remove most of the leaves from the hydrangea and submerge the whole flower in the water for about two hours.

Shake off the excess water.

Cut the stems to two inches longer than the depth of your container.

Place the hydrangeas in the water-filled container, placing the leaves around the edge.

Fold four-by-twelve-inch rectangles of heavy weight paper accordion–style and tape them to a wooden skewer.

Add four or five fans to the bouquet to finish.

Pinch off small segments of hydrangea and place them in small water tubes. Lay a row of flowers around each tier of the cake, hiding the tubes. Decorate the top with one hydrangea bloom (in a larger tube) and a bow with long streamers draped over the cake. This ribbon is two yards of two-inch-wide sheer organza.

The guest-book table is the first thing the guests will see when they arrive at the reception, and it deserves a flower arrangement. Keep it small and simple: two white hydrangeas in a little glazed-pottery vase (left).

herb centerpiece how-to

Herbs make a fragrant and lively arrangement for a casual or country summer centerpiece. A simple basket is the container.

Pin frog
Plastic liner
8 Stems thornless blackberry
10 Stems lavender
10 Stems marjoram
10 Stems flowering oregano
10 Stems ladies mantle
10 Stems catnip (which has tiny purple flowers)

☙ Set the pin frog in the liner and place it in the basket. Fill two-thirds with water.

☙ Arrange each of the herbs in bunches of 10 stems in your hand and trim the bottom evenly.
☙ Place the bunches of herbs around the edge of the basket by securing them in the frog.
☙ Place the lavender near the handle of the basket.

Early summer brings the sumptuous blooms of the tree peony, which the Chinese call "one hundred petals." Peonies bloom in many luscious shades of pink—just one flower in a vase will make a statement (above). A line of peonies, each flower in a small vase filled with pink glass marbles makes a beautiful centerpiece on a rectangular table. A four-inch-wide satin ribbon under the vases ties the look together and adds color.

I love pairing a vase with flowers in the same color. This golden-yellow ceramic container (right) holds 20 "Gold Medal" garden roses surrounded by a collar of six stems of these velvet-textured scented geranium leaves. I finished off the arrangement by adding some feather butterflies on wires from the craft store. The butterflies hovering above the roses add a very special touch to this warm summer bouquet.

fall

The colors of autumn are rich and warm, creating sumptuous tables to celebrate the bounty of harvest time. Centerpieces of bright yellow sunflowers and black-eyed Susans are cheerful and long-lasting when the light is fading and the landscape is catching fire with turning leaves. The incredible range of hot colors found in dahlias and chrysanthemums highlight any choice of dishes and glassware. Using golden magnolia leaves, fruit, and berries create a look of abundance for Thanksgiving; and the traditional orange marigold with deep red coxcomb for a "Day of the Dead" fiesta can be your inspiration for entertaining during the fall season.

provence:
a country table

In September, we can enjoy one last meal served

in *le beau soleil*—the beautiful sun—for this is Indian Summer, often the warmest time of year in California. A simple meal of soup, bread, wine, salad, cheese, and raspberries set in the greenhouse or on the patio could last all afternoon. The food is served casually on a bare table that doesn't take attention away from the unique French country dishes. A centerpiece is sometimes in the way of the food, but this bountiful arrangement of olive, lavender, and black-eyed Susans can be appreciated when placed to one side of the table.

Provence–inspired dishes with a warm ochre glaze are popular now and very inexpensive varieties can be found in many stores. A small *atelier* in Provence produces my mother's beautiful

Engobe earthenware. These handmade dishes are glazed in sun-drenched yellow and painted with garlands of leaves, olives, flowers, and fruit—*chaque a son gout*, "no two the same." The footed cups, *mazagrans*, take their name from a popular French hangover remedy of cold coffee and seltzer.

Provence was the inspiration for this centerpiece in its container made with French bread. I love the combination of olive and lavender and black-eyed Susans, whose bright-yellow petals and deep-purple centers are worthy of a van Gogh painting. Black-eyed Susan is in the aster family and is closely related to the medicinal echinacea. She is also called rudbeckia, named for a Swedish botanist who fathered 24 children and wrote the definitive illustrated volume listing all the plants known to scientists at the end of the seventeenth century. Rudbeckia has many varieties with wonderful names—"Bambi," "Goldilocks," "Toto," and "Irish Eyes."

centerpiece how-to

4 French bread baguettes
19" Plastic planter
A hot glue gun
Chicken wire
20 Stems of olive
18 Stems rudbeckia (black-eyed Susan)
10 Stems hypernicum berries
25 Stems lavender

🖎 Attach the flat bottom of two baguettes to each side of the planter using a very generous amount of hot glue. Apply the glue quickly and hold each loaf of bread firmly to the planter until the glue hardens.

🖎 Bend an 18- by 10-inch piece of chicken wire into a U-shape and fit it into the planter to create a grid across the top.

🖎 Cut the olive into several eight-inch and 10-inch sprigs. Insert the olive sprigs into the chicken wire covering the entire edge of the planter. Use the longer sprigs to drape over the exposed plastic ends of the container.

🖎 Cut the rudbeckia stems and place them across the top of the arrangement.

🖎 Cut the hypernicum to eight-inch pieces and fill in the spaces around the rudbeckia.

🖎 Add the lavender throughout the arrangement to finish.

dia de los muertos

a mexican halloween party

Our neighbors in Mexico celebrate the lives of those they loved and honor with a festival that mixes traditional Mesoamerican cultures and the Catholic All Soul's Day celebration. Mexicans believe in inviting the souls of the departed back to visit and bless them every year. *Dia de los Muertos* is really a three-day holiday, which begins October 31. For the people this festival holds the same importance as Christmas. It is not a morbid remembrance or a time for grief, but a joyous and life-affirming family reunion celebrated with music and bright flowers, food, and drink. There are parties at home and at the gravesite. Observing

Blanca belong to collector Nancy Armstrong. The *ocho micho* (a Mexican folk art sculpture of a taxi driven by the devil himself) and the green-and-black glazed dishes from Patzcuaro, Mexico, were loaned by Susan Pollard.

The historic adobe at the Westerbeke Ranch Conference Center in Sonoma California is the site of this *Dia de los Muertos* party. Papier-mâché skeletons (this fellow belongs to Amy Davis of Rancho Santa Fe) decorate homes and shops and are invited to join in the holiday feast. They can be found in any store in a Mexican neighborhood and are very inexpensive. Guests and family will share *mole*, *tamales*, and all the favorite foods of the departed ones. They will drink hot fruit punch, tequila, beer, and wine. The table is decorated with plenty of fruit and a path of marigold petals lit by traditional white candles to show the dead the way to the table.

Dia de los Muertos continues the bond between death and life, present and past. I loved learning about this fiesta and making a Mexican dinner party with the traditional elements of the holiday.

On the first night of the fiesta, the family welcomes visitors with cinnamon-spiced hot chocolate and *pan de muertos*, a loaf of sweet yeast bread decorated with the shapes of bones and tears. Children are offered sugar-paste skulls and candy coffins to let them know that death is not bitter, and to create a sweet association, rather than dread or fear.

The hand-woven tablecloth and whimsical ceramic opossum vase by Mexican artist Teodora

centerpiece how-to

Zempoalxuchitl (marigolds), which represent death, and blood-red coxcomb are the traditional *Dia de los Muertos* flowers. They decorate the *altar de muertos*, houses, and graves during the festival. Marigolds are native to Mexico and Central America. The seeds germinate in only a week, and the gardener is rewarded with flowers very soon after. Marigolds are planted as borders in French gardens as a snail barrier. The variety in this centerpiece is "Perfection Orange."

2 Dozen marigolds
Five-inch ceramic pot
8 Coxcomb flowers

✎ Clean the stems of the marigolds and cut them to about 10 inches.
✎ Arrange them in the pot by placing them one at a time opposite each other, crossing their stems.
✎ As you add marigolds in this way a grid is formed which anchors the flowers in a dome shape.
✎ Clean the stems of eight coxcomb flowers, leaving only a few leaves closest to the bloom.
✎ Tuck the coxcomb in a row around the edge of the pot forming a "collar" around the marigolds.

The candleholders and handmade pottery dishes made by renowned Mexican potter Georki Gonzales are from the collection of Patty Westerbeke and Nancy Armstrong of Sonoma. Plain pottery or terra-cotta plates would work just as well for your party. The fringed natural cotton napkins, flatware, wineglasses, and crystal glass are easily available.

The most important element of the holiday preparation is constructing the *altar de muertos* or *ofrenda*. The altar is placed on the dining room table or in an alcove in the living room. Everyone participates in making the *ofrenda* out of boxes covered with cloth or decorative paper to honor the "dead ones" and lure them home. At the top of my *ofrenda* is a statue of Our Lady of Guadalupe on a bed of marigold petals. She is surrounded by folk art candleholders in the shape of animals that will help to guide loved ones back to earth. I placed the tradi-

chose a baseball, phonograph records, and his rosary beads. A folkloric guardian angel and a skeleton singing and playing a guitar recall stories he told and songs he sang to me. My mother-in-law's turquoise necklace, a miniature replica of her favorite teapot, and books adorn her place, along with a little skeleton baker commemorating her delicious cookies, cakes, and pies. My beloved great-aunt is encouraged to visit by the skeleton hairdresser, high heels (which were her passion), and the roses she loved to grow. The "dead ones" are given a glass of water to quench their thirst when they arrive.

tional dish of salt on the altar representing both purification and the spice of life.

The corners of the *ofrenda* are guarded by fantastic sugar skulls decorated with foil and bright-colored frosting. The base is covered with the elaborate cutout tissue-paper banners called *papel picado*. Amy Davis contributed the humorous little skeletons dressed to represent the occupations of the family. Offerings of fancy bread and sugar skulls are placed in front of the altar to nourish the "dead ones" after their journey. My *ofrenda* is surrounded by candles to light their way back home.

The second level displays the pictures of my departed family members and miniature representations of the things they loved in life. For my father, I

asian lunch

One beautiful plate or piece of fabric can be the inspiration for your table. Highlight a treasure with complementing or contrasting color and complete the setting with neutral and inexpensive dishes. The inspiration for this luncheon table was the luminous and delicate jade rice bowls my mother bought during a wonderful trip we took together to Hong Kong. My friend Susy offered me her green antique Japanese silk obi, and I was dazzled by the gorgeous hand-painted green and apricot butterflies and chrysanthemums. The mums, I decided, would have to be my centerpiece flowers. I bought three yards of apricot-colored chiffon to cover the table and added two small arrangements of persimmons—an autumn treat much favored by the Chinese. Susy also contributed two very old and valuable deities, one Chinese, one Thai. I added a brass Japanese Buddha belonging to my neighbor and my own Buddhas from Indonesia and Thailand, to decorate Genny and Gerry Wilson's Sea Ranch dining room.

A classic Chinese meal begins with soup served in a bowl, which may also be used for rice after the soup is eaten. Plates are small, as each dish is eaten in turn, one at a time. Everyone is provided with a tea bowl, chopsticks, a bowl for rice, and small dishes for soy sauce and condiments such as hot mustard and plum sauce. A very formal meal would also include fancy rests for the chopsticks, a serving spoon, a dish for fish bones, and a tiny cup for the wine, which is served warm.

Chopsticks are made of bamboo, wood, plastic, precious coral, jade, ivory, or even silver or gold. Chinese say that food tastes better when eaten with chopsticks. Every bite can be enjoyed and the sauce can never drown the flavor of the food. Since only a few morsels can be picked up at a time, the tempo of the meal is more relaxed. Chopsticks can move with such speed and nimbleness that the Chinese name for them means "quick little boys."

The celadon plates belong to the Wilsons, but the inexpensive dishes, cups, and butterfly chopstick rests were all found in San Francisco's Chinatown. The elements of the table include several Asian cultures, but the large plates and the napkins are strictly Western.

centerpiece how-to

The Buddha sits on a pillow made from orange chrysanthemums set on an oriental pedestal.
You will need:

One block of green floral foam
Shallow four-inch plastic dish
Waterproof green florist's tape
25 chrysanthemum stems with multiple flowers
Small Buddha statue and pedestal

🍃 Cut the floral foam in half and trim the corners.
🍃 Soak the foam in water for two hours, and then place it in the dish.
🍃 Secure the foam to the dish with the tape.
🍃 Cut the stems of the mums to one and a half inches and stick them into the foam, covering it completely with flowers. Leave a space the size of the statue's base on the top.
🍃 Place the Buddha on the flower pillow and set both on the pedestal.
The centerpiece will last at least a week.

Chrysanthemum means "golden flower." This Chinese symbol for autumn and harvest is also the pictorial symbol for longevity and health. Mums represent royalty in Japan. The rising sun in the Japanese flag is also a chrysanthemum, and the Japanese seat of royalty is called "The Chrysanthemum Throne."

thanksgiving

Our family gathers at my house every Thanksgiving.

I cook the turkey and everyone brings something, which is often exactly the same dish as the year before, and the year before that. We like tradition. We find comfort in some things staying the same. We always have soup in my mother's pressed-glass turkeys and dinner on my mother-in-law's 1950s Apple dishes. Sometimes I borrow Apple dishes from my friend, Deborah, who inherited hers, just as I did. We go around the table and each give thanks for our own blessings of the year. Bathed in candlelight, the table is warm, crowded, and cozy—like my family.

I took a plate with me to shop for a new table covering that would match the green and the burgundy red in my dishes. I found the perfect colors in a piece of upholstery fabric. We have so much more choice with fabrics than ready-made table linens. The dishes are Franciscan pottery in the "Apple" pattern made in California during the first half of the 1900s. Like Fiestaware, it costs very little, and is still available. The branch flatware is mine. The cake stand holding the centerpiece, the fringed off-white napkins, matte-brass napkin rings, highball glass, and the pumpkin-shaped wineglasses are all new.

The dishes are the same, but I do make a different centerpiece each year. I always incorporate this little pressed paper-and-pinecone turkey. This year he sits atop a pyramid of autumn fruits, miniature white pumpkins, velvety magnolia leaves, and snowberries. Native Americans call snowberries "famine food" because they are edible, but taste like bitter soap. Snowberry, also called waxberry, or wolfberry, is in the honeysuckle family. Hummingbirds and bees love their nectar. Bees produce a pale, almost-clear honey from its pink flowers in summer.

centerpiece how-to

To construct this pyramid you will need:

12-inch Styrofoam cone
Florist's clay
12- to 14-inch Square cake stand or platter
Wooden skewers
6 Large and 10 small red delicious apples
12 Pomegranates
10 Miniature white pumpkins
40 Magnolia leaves
Toothpicks
2 Bunches of Snowberries (20)

Step 1

- Cut the top two inches off the cone.
- Put a generous strip of clay on the plate and stick the Styrofoam securely to the center.
- Break some skewers in half and stick them halfway into one side of the largest apples and pomegranates and four of the pumpkins.
- Attach the fruit to the Styrofoam cone by sticking the end of the skewer into the base of the cone, alternating apple, pomegranate, and pumpkin along the edge of the plate.

Step 2

- Arrange a row of magnolia leaves under the first row of fruits.
- Next, cut a notch in the stem end of the remaining magnolia leaves and attach them in a row above the fruit by pinning the notched end to the Styrofoam cone with two toothpicks.
- Add another row of fruit as instructed above, add more leaves, then smaller fruit, until you have covered the cone with the fruit and leaves.
- Cut the clusters of snowberries from their branches. Tuck the berries into the spaces between the fruit to fill any holes.
- Top the pyramid with a piece of fruit, a Thanksgiving decoration, or a small bunch of snowberries to finish.

barn wedding

The Sea Ranch Lodge on the Northern California coast

near the tiny town of Gualala is the rustic setting for this autumn wedding. Rays of late-afternoon sun pierce the weathered boards of the old barn overlooking the Pacific. Guests are seated at long banquet tables for the sunset reception dinner, to be followed by dancing and chocolate wedding cake. The atmosphere is nostalgic as well as warm and intimate. Copper charger plates glow in the light from votive candles—one for every guest. The flames are reflected in a row of jewel-colored antique bottles, each one holding dahlia blooms of deep purple and hot-sunset colors. The bottles are the collection of my friend Bob, who has been digging in former dumpsites all over northern California for 25 years and has an incredible assortment of old bottles in beautiful blue, aqua, green, lavender, amber, and rich-brown glass.

Dahlias bloom in late summer and early autumn. They are a native of Mexico, called *cocoxochitl*, which the Aztecs used for food. When the Conquistadors took dahlias back to Spain in the sixteenth century they caused a sensation among Europeans who hated their peppery taste, but were passionate about the blooms. Spain has a holiday called Day of the Dahlia. The dahlias on this table are an exciting collection of varieties in orange, peach, yellow, and purple. One single dahlia bloom is so spectacular it can be used by itself.

The bottles are placed in a row on a long table, but on a round or square table they can be grouped on a mirror or tray surrounded by angel vine or leaves. If you want to create this look but do not have access to such a collection, most antique shops have old bottles for sale. Or you can use inexpensive glass bud vases instead. Add a few drops of food coloring to tint the water any shade you choose to complement your theme.

Rental companies are a boon to the hostess for a large party or wedding. The many choices they offer today make it possible to create a variety of great-looking table settings. This reception's copper tablecloths and napkins, tables, natural wood chairs, flatware, clear glass dishes, and crystal wine glasses, including goblets and champagne flutes, are all rented. The chargers and napkin rings were made for less than five dollars for each place setting.

setting how-to

∼ The chargers under the glass plates are inexpensive 12-inch pizza pans that I sprayed with copper paint.

∼ To create a richer patina I sponged on a thin coat of metallic-copper craft paint and sealed it with a light coat of spray lacquer.

∼ The napkin rings double as a keepsake for each guest. I tied the chain around the napkins to add more sparkle to the table setting.

∼ They are made from a copper chain tipped with glass beads the same colors as the bottles that decorate the table. You can buy supplies at bead or craft shops.

∼ Cut the chain into eight-inch lengths with wire cutters and attach the beads to each end with a two-inch piece of 20-gauge copper wire, curling the wire at the end to keep the beads from sliding off.

alternate centerpieces how-to

Sunflowers

Another centerpiece for a casual or country autumn wedding is this cheery arrangement of golden sunflowers and chocolate cosmos. *Cosmos* is the Greek word for "beautiful." Sunflowers were revered by the Incas, who made images of the flower in hammered gold for their temples. They were amazed by how the sunflower turned to face the sun as it moves across the sky. Every part of the sunflower is useful: the oil from the seeds for eating, cooking, and making soap and cosmetics; the leaves for cloth; and the stalks for animal fodder.

15 Sunflowers
Flower pail six-inches deep with a five-inch opening
18 Chocolate cosmos
Florist wire
Spraymount glue
ribbon

❦ Cut the stems of the sunflowers to eight inches.

❦ Place sunflowers around the rim of the pail.

❦ Fill in the center of the bouquet with the rest of the sunflowers.

❦ Trim the stems of chocolate cosmos flowers to nine inches and add them into the arrangement so they appear to hover above the sunflowers.

❦ The table number is very simple to create with florist wire bent into the shape of the number. Leave about 10 inches of wire at the bottom to stand the table number in the bouquet.

❦ Fold and bend a piece of five-eighths- to one-inch-wide ribbon into the shape of the number; apply spray mount glue.

❦ Place the wire number on top and cover it with another piece of ribbon formed into the shape of the number.

❦ Press the two ribbons together sealing the wire between them. It takes from 12 to 34 inches of ribbon to construct each digit.

Roses

A more elegant centerpiece for fall is a frosted-glass or metal vase brimming with a generous display of Leonidas roses. Leonidas is a gorgeous hybrid rose, which appeared in flower markets only a few years ago. Its caramel-copper color makes it very popular, especially in autumn.

18 or 20 Leonidas roses
10-inch-tall Vase with a five-inch opening

❦ Clean the stems of leaves except those closest to the flower.

❦ Make a fresh cut in the rose stems under water and arrange them in the vase one at a time.

❦ Place the roses opposite one another, alternating from each of the four sides of the vase. This creates a grid that will support the flowers as you position them in the center of the arrangement.

winter

Winter is the most traditional party season, from Christmas and New Year's Eve to a celebration for lovers on Valentine's Day. While we usually think of evergreens, holly, and mistletoe for decorating the table in winter, remember there are huge red amaryllis, blue delphinium, and orange lilies in the flower market too. And at the end of winter nature gives us the beautiful tulip as a preview of spring. Be imaginative with holiday decorations. Use Christmas ornaments in new ways, metallic accents, and winter whites. Enhance your china and sparkling crystal with a glittering centerpiece or liven the table with bright contrasting colors.

british

colonial table

Vibrant and contrasting colors are a dramatic theme for a table: yellow with purple, pink with green, or red with turquoise. Use dishes and linens that contrast and accent them with candles and flowers in the same tones. My mother's British–export print fabric is a great background for her English porcelain with its classic "Blue Willow" pattern. The color contrast of cobalt blue and tangerine orange repeats in the flowers, creating a striking table.

British merchants, diplomats, and military lived on every continent. They adopted the art and style of the cultures they colonized, and brought them into their own homes. English mills duplicated and exported Indian fabric designs all over the world. Carvings and pictures of exotic animals were popular souvenirs of Africa. "Blue Willow" porcelain came to England from China during the eighteenth century, and at one time or another for two hundred years, every British

pottery company has manufactured this familiar blue-and-white china.

The pictures painted on the china tell the story of a mandarin's daughter who was imprisoned in a little fenced house beneath a willow tree because she fell in love with a commoner. Her beloved rescued her and they ran away, carrying her box of jewels. Her enraged father followed them across the bridge, but they escaped from him in a small boat. The couple lived on a tiny island until the father discovered their house and set it on fire, burning them to death. The gods took pity on

the lovers and turned them into two doves flying toward the place of eternal happiness together.

The "Blue Willow" china is my mother's everyday set of dishes. The pattern is complemented by gold–trimmed flatware and blue glasses.

Greet guests with flowers in your entryway. An extravagant bouquet that duplicates the color of your table arrangement creates your theme right at the beginning of the evening. Twenty stems of delphinium and 15 eye-popping orange Asiatic lilies are complemented beautifully by a vase in the same sapphire blue as the flowers.

Blue flowers are very prized in the garden and a favorite of butterflies. Belladonna, or delphinium, is available all year long, and forget-me-nots pop up as early as December in places where the ground does not freeze. There is a story that Adam had finished naming all the animals and all the plants when this modest little blue flower called out, "Forget me not!" Adam was out of ideas, so her plea became her name.

centerpiece how-to

Serving pieces can make excellent containers for table bouquets. This centerpiece is a soup tureen holding bright orange and blue flowers. Make a grid with sticky green florist's tape across the opening of a wide container, attaching the tape to the edges one and a half inches apart.

18 Stems euphorbia
24 Stems dark-blue delphinium (belladonna)
12 Orange Asiatic lilies
24 Stems forget-me-nots

☙ Begin with 12 euphorbia. Remove most of the leaves and cut the stems to fit your container. Space them evenly around the edge, so they drape over the rim.
☙ Add the delphinium, filling the spaces between the euphorbia. Insert the rest of the delphinium across the grid, filling your container.
☙ Cut the lilies to no more than twice the depth of your container. Place them all around your arrangement. (Be aware that the pollen will stain your clothes and table linens, so you may wish to remove it.)
☙ Add the remaining euphorbia throughout the middle of the bouquet.

☙ Remove most of the leaves from the forget-me-nots and put them into any spaces between the flowers in little bunches of three flowers.

This centerpiece will last up to two weeks if every day or two you put the arrangement in the sink and flood with clean water until the old water is replaced.

ice:
a table of crystal and glass

Most couples register their choice of china, glassware, and flatware with a department store before sending the wedding invitations. And many of us decide to buy "good china" at a later time in our lives, perhaps when we can afford it. Today there are hundreds of designs to choose from in every style and price range. Pick china you love from the many classic patterns available or more modern pieces from world-famous designers such as Calvin Klein, Versace, Kate Spade, and the simply elegant Vera Wang. Don't put your dishes and silver away to save it just for special occasions, bring it out to enjoy whenever you want a little glamour, even if it is only a dinner for the two of you.

centerpiece how-to

A sand-blasted manzanita branch from the craft store is sprayed with a pearl glaze and dusted with clear glitter to represent a bare frost-covered tree set in a baby's breath snowbank.

2 Blocks floral foam
1 Low-sided glass container (this one is 10 inches square)
Sticky florist tape
24 Stems baby's breath
Floral tape
1 Manzanita branch (sandblasted so that the bark is removed)
Pearl spray glaze
Spray glue
Clear glitter

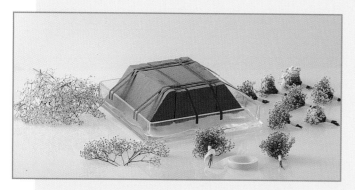

Soak the floral foam in water for two hours.

Slice one block lengthwise on the diagonal and fit it into your container on either side of the whole piece, with the cut sides facing outward.

Secure the foam to the edges of the container with the sticky tape.

Cut three-inch long clusters of baby's breath from their main stems and make 30 tight little bunches, wrapping them with the florist tape and leaving the ends exposed. Pull the tape as you wrap, it sticks to itself when stretched.

Cut the ends of the stems on an angle to make it easy to stick into the foam.

Spray the branch with the pearl glaze.

When the glaze is dry spray the branch with glue and generously sprinkle with the glitter.

Position the branch by pushing it firmly into the center of the foam.

Cover the foam with bunches of baby's breath, overlapping the edges of your container.

The arrangement will last for more than a week.

A winter dinner party or New Year's Eve celebration at home is an opportunity to lay a gorgeous table with your best china and a few Christmas ornaments for decoration. This icy theme is created with silver-trimmed white dishes, glass candelabra, a sheer sparkly tablecloth, and snowflakes hung from the dining room ceiling.

The simple-to-create bare-branch centerpiece completes a glittering winter scene.

The champagne flutes, wineglasses, and dishes all have a contemporary design. The cut-glass candelabra with a crystal tree topper in the center, stainless flatware, and the crystal snowflakes hanging above the table provide the sparkle.

One I love
two I love
three I love I say,

valentine's day party

When you design a theme table, don't hold back.

As long as you stay with one or two colors, you can mix several styles and be lavish with accessories. Ruby-red dishes and glasses on a white paper doily, red and white candy boxes, heart-tipped stirrers, a white bowl filled with ripe red strawberries, and napkins trimmed with crocheted lace create the look of fancy paper valentines. A milk-glass cake stand heaped with *petits fours*, little cakes decorated with hearts and flowers, is the final detail on a beautiful table for Valentine's Day. I used small clear-plastic stand-up picture frames to display a charming antique valentine at each place. Boxes covered with shiny red wrapping paper and decorated with more valentines hold red tulips— the perfect flowers to go with the hearts.

Clear-glass dishes are a valuable staple for entertaining and can be mixed with the color or

pattern on your salad or dessert plates. These clear plates are perfect with the 1950's ruby glass dishes and cups I have collected over the years from flea markets and garage sales.

I would rather have red tulips than roses on Valentine's Day. They look so joyful and let us know that spring is on its way. In the romantic Victorian flower language, the tulip is a declaration of love and means "perfect love" and "perfect lover." To give tulips on the most romantic day of the year is to give your sweetheart the right message in a lovely bouquet.

centerpiece how-to

5 Dozen tulips (24 tulips for each four-inch container, and 36 for the six-inch)
3 Rubber bands
2 Four-inch-high vases
1 Six-inch-high vase
2 Gift boxes four- by four- by six-inches
1 Gift box four- by four- by eight-inches
Wrapping paper to cover the boxes
Double-sided tape
4 Valentines for each box

🍃 Begin with a tulip in your hand, and then add tulips close to each other in a spiral pattern until you have a dome-shaped bouquet.

🍃 Wrap a rubber band around the stems to hold them in place.

🍃 Cut the stems to the height of your container with a sharp knife because scissors or clippers will crush the stems.

🍃 Place the tulips in water in the vase.

🍃 The container is a simple cardboard box wrapped neatly in gift paper held in place with double-sided tape. Attach a valentine to every side of the box with a piece of the tape, and place the vase of tulips inside.

christmas wedding

Christmastime is the second most popular time of year for a marriage ceremony. A Christmas Eve wedding has been considered good luck since Colonial times because, according to folklore, angels may attend. Snow on your wedding day means you will have lots of money in your future together. Your decorations can be in a holiday theme of traditional red and green or an elegant combination of winter white and silver or gold.

A Christmas ornament with the guest's name (written with glitter paint from the craft store) is the place card as well as the party favor and keepsake of a wedding or holiday party. Use a small piece of double-sided tape under the ornament to keep it in place on the plate. The tables, chairs, place settings, and the green linens with sheer gold overlay, create an elegant look for the reception, and, surprisingly, are all standard rental items.

centerpiece how-to

These elegant topiaries are easy to create with red or white roses and Christmas greens, holly, or mistletoe. In ancient times, the Druids revered mistletoe because it grows without roots as if it fell from heaven. They gathered the leaves by cutting it from trees with a ceremonial gold knife and catching the falling branches in a pure white cloth. The Druids hung the sprigs in doorways to protect the home from lightning and as a symbol of peace and hospitality. Mistletoe was used in solstice celebrations—hence its connection to the Christian winter holiday.

Four-inch floral foam ball
1 Five- to six-inch heavy flowerpot
Plaster of Paris
15-inch-long Bamboo garden stake, or a straight branch or stick, or a one-half-inch-thick clear plastic dowel

1 Small water tube
20 Long stems of mistletoe cut into three-inch-long pieces.
12 Roses
24 inches Decorative ribbon
Mood moss or sheet moss

The mistletoe will last for a week in the foam, so the topiaries can be made well in advance. Just add the roses on the day before the event.

᧖ Soak the foam ball in water for two hours, and then remove it to drain for two hours so it won't drip on your table.

᧖ Push the empty water tube into the ball so that its lip is even with the surface. This prevents the stick from going all the way through the foam ball.

᧖ Fill the pot with plaster (prepared according to package directions) to one inch from the top.

᧖ Place the stick into the center and secure with tape or hold it until the plaster sets, being sure it is perfectly straight.

᧖ Decorate the ball with the pieces of mistletoe by pushing them firmly into the foam until its entire surface is evenly covered.

᧖ Cut the rose stems to three inches and push them into the ball about four inches apart.

᧖ When the plaster is set, insert the top of the stick into the water tube.

᧖ Tie a ribbon on the stick close to the bottom of the ball.

᧖ Cover the plaster with the moss to finish.

candleholder how-to

Simple snowball candleholders made of white carnations trimmed with sprigs of holly are reminiscent of the seasonal coconut-covered ice cream snowballs we loved as children. They are easy to make and are a whimsical centerpiece for a Christmas party or wedding.

1 floral foam ball (Available in 4 or 6 inches. The 4-inch ball requires 40–45 carnations, the 6-inch requires 60–70.
1 Small saucer
Carnations
1 Candle
2–3 sprigs of holly for each snowball

Slice off a small section of the ball so it will sit flat on the saucer.

Soak the ball in water for two hours, and then remove it to drain for two hours so it won't drip on your table.

Cut the carnation stems to two inches and push them as far as you can into the ball. You can make a hole in the foam with your finger to fit the thick green base of the flower deeper into the foam.

Cover the entire surface of the foam with flowers, leaving a space for the candle on the top.

Add the candle by pushing it securely into the foam. Cut the holly and push the stems into the ball close to the candle to finish.

A potted amaryllis is a spectacular flower for a table decoration, and one of the few flowers that bloom in the heart of winter. The plant is a native of the Cape of Good Hope, named for the Greek *amaryssein*, which means "to shine." In the Victorian flower language, amaryllis means "pride," and "splendid beauty."

For a shining holiday centerpiece I decorated the amaryllis with a string of glass Christmas-tree beads. I secured the beads at the top with a straight pin and wrapped it around the length of the stem.

tools & supplies

Any flower arrangement can be constructed using a sharp knife and scissors and (*bottom, left to right*) a lopping shear or pruner for cutting woody stems and branches, a clipper or bunch cutter for stems, and a wire cutter.

(*top, left to right*)
Green floral foam, adhesive floral clay, cloth bowl tape a.k.a. sticky green tape, florist stem wrap tape, and pin frogs.
(*bottom, left to right*)
Wooden skewers, rubber bands, U-pins (fern pins), water tubes, and water picks (pointed).

source guide

You will be able to find many of the items I used on these tables from national chain stores like Macys and Crate & Barrel in your hometown, or through their web sites listed below. I encourage you to investigate your local party-rental company. Most items are standard and the choices are so much greater than they used to be. My friends and family generously loaned me dishes and accessories, but some of the things I used were ordered online or purchased at discount and import stores.

Dessert Buffet
Pages 2, 4: "Grand Buffet" cups and coffee pot, Lenox "Monroe" champagne glasses available at Macys or on www.macys.com. Bavarian china dessert plates from my collection. Glacé fruit arrangement from Fauchon, 442 Park Avenue, New York NY 10022, (212) 308-5919, or www.fauchon.com.

SPRING
Pages 8–9: Opener: "Jacqueline" tulips can be ordered from mid-January to mid-February from www.citywreaths.com.

Birds: A Spring Celebration
Pages 10, 11, 12: Antique transferware salad plates "Faience Anglaise Grand Depot de Porcelaines & Faiences" from the collection of Susan Pollard. Lenox "British Colonial" dinner plates, Lenox "Laurel Leaf" linens, Villory & Boch "Boston" goblets, and Wallace "Gold Accent Corsica" flatware from Macys, or www.macys.com. Blue and green wineglasses and champagne flutes from Ross Stores (about a dollar apiece). 1930's hand painted mirror-backed place cards from my collection.

Page 15: Green Victorian wire baskets from the collection of Linda Sunshine. Antique transfer ware serving pieces "Faience Anglaise Grand Depot de Porcelaines & Faiences" from the collection of Susan Pollard.

Afternoon Tea
Page 17, 18: Tablecloth from Hertz Party Rents, 5750 Paradise Dr., Corte Madera, CA 94925, (415) 924-4444. Branch coral teapot and cups from the collection of Ruth Miska. Ceramic serving pieces from Crate & Barrel or www.crateandbarrel.com.

Page 19 *left*: Teapot, vintage china cups, napkins, antique spoons from the collection of Diane Kelly.

Page 19 *right*: Fiestaware dishes from my collection, purchased at flea markets. Napkins made by my grandmother in the 1940s. Spoons from Ikea, or www.ikea.com.

Page 20: Silver teapot, creamer, and sugar bowl from the collection of Diane Kelly.

Page 21: "Madison" tea set from Crate & Barrel, or www.crateandbarrel.com.

***Rose*: A Pink Table**
Pages 22, 24: Limoge china from the collection of Diane Kelly. Fostoria etched crystal glasses, "Rose Print" Wallace sterling silverware from the collection of Barbara Young.

Mother's Day & Father's Day
Pages 27, 28: Hand-painted plates by Samantha Stevens. Fabric paint, tablecloth supplies from Ben Franklin Crafts. Cups, juice glasses, sugar bowl, creamer from Cost Plus, or www.costplusworldmarket.com.

"Share-the-Wealth" Wedding
Pages 30–31: Tables, chairs, green tablecloths from Hertz Party Rents, 5750 Paradise Dr., Corte Madera, CA 94925, (415) 924-4444.

Page 32: Bauer pottery plates, pink Depression glass wine & water glasses, antique damask linens, McCoy vase from the collection of Lena Tabori.

Page 33: "Orient" china by Noritake, loaned by Sarah Fairchild. Bamboo napkin rings from Macys, or www.macys.com. "Kyoto" flatware, natural woven place mats, parchment napkins, "Silhouette" champagne flutes, "Rita" wineglasses from Crate & Barrel, or www.crateandbarrel.com. Hand-made bamboo box for centerpiece from Claudia Allin Designs, Novato CA, (415) 892-5292.

Page 34: Franciscan "Ivy" dishes, napkins, tablecloth from my collection (dishes can be found through www.replacements.com). "Calistoga" glassware from Crate & Barrel, or www.crateandbarrel.com. Branch flatware from FLAX Art & Design, or www.flaxmart.com.

Page 35: "Black Fantasy" china from the collection of Cathy Obiedo. Matte silver chargers from Costco, or www.costco.com. Tablecloth and napkins from Hertz Party Rents, 5750 Paradise Dr., Corte Madera, CA 94925, (415) 924-4444. "Oona" stainless flatware, "Renoir" champagne flutes from Crate & Barrel, or www.crateandbarrel.com. Vase for centerpiece from Restoration Hardware, or www.restorationhardware.com.

Page 36: Lenox cutwork linens, Wedgwood "India" china, "Golden Ribbon" flatware, "Marque" goblets and flutes from Macy's Bridal Registry, or www.macys.com. Metal box for centerpiece from my collection.

Page 37: Depression glass dessert dishes, cake stand from the collection of Lena Tabori. Antique embroidered tablecloth was made by my mother & grandmother.

SUMMER
Pages 38–39: See pages 44–45; Treasure: Elegant Entertaining.

Americana: A Holiday Picnic
Pages 40–42: Enamel-ware containers, dish towels from Cost Plus, or www.costplusworldmarket.com. Flatware from Ikea, or www.ikea.com. Sand pails, tin berry buckets from Coast Floral Supply San Francisco CA, (415) 777-8533.

Page 43 *lower right*:
Plastic-box photo frames: Aaron Brothers, www.aaronbrothers.com. Floral foam: craft & floral supply store.

Treasure: Elegant Entertaining
Pages 44–45: Indian sari silk chair covers, mirrored table covering (curtain panel) from Kate Geddes Design, Mill Valley CA, (415) 381-7183. Wine glasses, Wedgwood "Gold Florentine" china from the collection of Diane Kelly. Faux-gold flatware from Ross Stores (four place settings for ten dollars). Mirror tiles from Home Depot, or www.homedepot.com.

Pages 46–47: Roses from Garden Valley Ranch, 498 Pepper Road, Petaluma CA 94952, or www.gardenvalley.com. Fabric glue, faux jewels, floral foam from craft & floral supply store.

Kauai: A Tropical Experience
Pages 48–49, 50, 51: Palm tree candlesticks, "Wicker" dinner plates, Lenox "British Colonial" salad plates and etched crystal glasses from Macys, or www.macys.com. Dendrobium orchid lei from Ikaika Exotics, or www.ikaikaexotics.com. Seashells, pineapple votives, wahini candles, dashboard hula dolls are souvenirs from Hawaii. Bamboo flatware, paper window blind from Cost Plus, or www.costplusworldmarket.com. Raffia hula skirts from Hertz Party Rents. Napkin fabric from The Kapaia Stitchery, 3-3551 Kuhio Hwy., Lihue HI 96766, (808) 245-2281.

Children's Birthday Party
Pages 52, 53: Paper plates, napkins, plastic cups, forks and spoons, "Crazy Straws" from Target, or www.target.com.

Page 55, *lower right*: "Daisy" cake plate from my collection.

White Summer Wedding
Pages 56–57, 58: Tables, chairs, chair covers, table linens, flatware, glasses, and square white plates from Hertz Party Rents, 5750 Paradise Dr., Corte Madera, CA 94925, (415) 924-4444. Fans from Cost Plus, or www.costplusworldmarket.com. Topper tablecloths, glazed-pottery vase (on guest book table) from my collection from flea markets and family.

Page 61 *top*: Vases, pink glass marbles, satin ribbon from Shibata Floral Supply, San Francisco CA, (415) 543-9880.

Page 61 *bottom*: Container, feather butterflies from Coast Floral Supply, San Francisco CA, (415) 777-8533.

FALL
Pages 62–63: See page 82; Barn Wedding.

Provence: A Country Table
Pages 64–65, 66: Engobe earthenware dishes from French Country Living catalog, 5568 West Chester Road, West Chester OH 45069, (800) 485-1302. "Charlemagne" flatware, "Logan" goblets from Crate & Barrel, or www.crateandbarrel.com. Napkins from Cost Plus, or www.costplusworldmarket.com.

Page 67: 19-inch plastic planter from Ikea, or www.ikea.com.

Dia de los Muertos: A Mexican Halloween Party
Page 70: Tablecloth, cups, ceramic opossum vase by Mexican artist Teodora Blanca from the collection of Nancy Armstrong. Patzcuaro plates, Ocho micho (Mexican folk art sculpture) from the collection of Susan Pollard.

Pages 71, 72: Cotton napkins, "Grand Hotel" flatware, "Verona Sapphire" wineglasses, and "Rita" crystal glasses from Crate & Barrel, or www.crateandbarrel.com. Folk art candleholders, pottery dishes by Georki Gonzales from the collections of Patty Westerbeke and Nancy Armstrong. Papier-mâché skeletons from Amy Davis Design, P.O. Box 675338, Rancho Santa Fe CA 92067, (858) 232-0098.

Page 73: Ofrenda: Our Lady of Guadalupe statue, folk art candleholders from the collections of Nancy Armstrong and Patty Westerbeke. Skeletons from Amy Davis Design, P.O. Box 675338, Rancho Santa Fe CA, 92067, (858) 232-0098. Sugar skulls from John Kelly & Associates Design Firm 126 13th Street Del Mar, CA 92014-2332, (858) 481-3488, www.johnkellydesign.com. Papel picado, (cutout tissue paper banners) from Eclipse de Mexico, 18615 Sonoma Hwy. #110, Sonoma CA 95476, (707) 939 3914.

Asian Lunch
Pages 75, 76: Antique Japanese silk obi, Asian deities statues from the collection of Susan Pollard. Jade rice bowls from collection of Diane Kelly. Celedon plates from the collection of Genny Wilson. Dinner plates from Macys, or www.macys.com. Tea bowls, wine cups, soup spoons, condiment dishes, chopsticks, chopstick rests were purchased at various Chinatown variety stores, also available in imports stores.

Thanksgiving
Page 78, 80: "Colby" highball glasses, "Annie" optic wineglasses, napkins, matte-brass napkin rings from Crate & Barrel, or www.crateandbarrel.com. Pressed glass turkeys were originally from Williams Sonoma. I added to my own collection by searching at www.ebay.com. Franciscan Apple dishes from my collection and Deborah Wunderlich's (older pieces can be found through www.replacements.com and new editions of this pattern can be found at Macys and other department stores that carry Franciscan Ware). Branch flatware from FLAX Art & Design, or www.flaxmart.com.

Page 81: Cake stand from Crate & Barrel, or www.crateandbarrel.com.

Barn Wedding
Pages 82–83, 85: Tables, natural-wood chairs, copper linens, flatware, glass dishes, crystal wineglasses, goblets, champagne flutes from Hertz Party Rents, 5750 Paradise Dr., Corte Madera, CA 94925, (415) 924-4444. Antique bottles from the collection of Bob Albachten (can be found in antique stores, flea markets). Chargers: craft paint, copper spray paint from craft store. Napkin rings: copper chain, wire, glass beads from Baubles & Beads, 1104 4th

Street, San Rafael CA 94901, (415) 457-8891. Cake from Let Them Eat Cake, Gualala CA (707) 884-1227.

Page 86: 5-inch pail from Coast Floral Supply, San Francisco CA, (415) 777-8533. Wire ribbon from Shibata Floral Supply, San Francisco CA, (415) 543-9880.

Page 87:
Vase: Shibata Floral Supply, San Francisco CA, (415) 543-9880.

WINTER
Pages 88–89: See page 95, Ice: A Table of Crystal and Glass.

British Colonial Table
Pages 90, 92: Burleigh Ware "Blue Willow" dishes from the collection of Diane Kelly (many versions of "Blue Willow." are available in stores from Gumps to Cost Plus in every price range). Lenox 'Federal Gold' flatware, Villory & Boch "Boston" goblets from Macys, or www.macys.com. Lantern candle holders from Cost Plus, or www.costplusworldmarket.com.

Page 93: Burleigh Ware "Blue Willow" soup tureen from the collection of Diane Kelly.

Ice: A Table of Crystal and Glass
Pages 95, 97: "Classic" champagne flutes, "Grosgrain" wineglasses and dishes by Vera Wang for Wedgwood, napkin rings, candelabra, Villeroy & Boch "New Wave" stainless flatware, Swarovski tree topper, Swarovski crystal snowflakes from Macys, or www.macys.com. Bead snowflakes by Anne Baldocchi Design, annebaldocchi@aol.com.

Valentine's Day Party
Pages 98–99, 100 *left*: Petits fours from Divine Delights, 1250 Holm Road Petaluma CA 94954, (707) 559-7099, or www.divinedelights.com. Antique Valentines, napkins from the collection of Susan Pollard. 1950's ruby-red dishes, cups, and glasses from my collection found at flea markets. Candy boxes, glass plates (cost $1.99) from Target, or www.target.com. Heart-tipped stirrers, striped glasses from Pier 1 Imports, or www.pier1.com. Milk-glass cake stand from the collection of Diane Kelly.

Pages 99–101: Antique Valentines from the collection of Susan Pollard.

Christmas Wedding
Pages 102–03, 104-105: Tables, Chiavari chairs, dishes, glassware, flatware, tablecloths and sheer gold overlay from Hertz Party Rents, 5750 Paradise Dr., Corte Madera, CA 94925, (415) 924-4444.

thank you to ...

My mother, Diane Kelly, who inspired me, encouraged me, taught me about entertaining with style, and loaned me so many of the wonderful dishes, linens, and glassware on these tables. She was a source of ideas and unconditional support throughout the process. I couldn't have done this book without her.

My husband, Floyd Heckman, for all his ideas and hard work.

Paul Prestidge for working like a slave on so many photo shoots.

Natasha Fried at Welcome for her support and suggestions.

Claudia Allin, my dear sister, who worked with me tirelessly and cheerfully on every table, adding her artistry to her labor, and making an enormous contribution to our work.

A creative and generous friend, Susan Pollard, who contributed so many ideas and let me borrow numerous treasures from her precious collections.

Hertz Party Rents, Corte Madera, California, who generously provided excellent quality tables, chairs, linens, and tableware for all the weddings. Their manager, Suzie Bradley, and her staff, who were so helpful in the production of this book.

Crate & Barrel, Corte Madera, California, loaned me countless dishes, glasses, flatware, and accessories, and their manager, Connie Brown, who had terrific ideas and helped me with so many of the tables.

Macys California and Suzanne Rodgers and the other wonderful women in the Fine China Department of the San Rafael, California, store, who were so creative and attentive in putting together many of the most beautiful settings in the book.

The Sea Ranch Lodge, The Sea Ranch, California.

Westerbeke Ranch & Conference Center, Sonoma, California.

The many friends who loaned me their dining rooms: Patty Westerbeke & Nancy Armstrong, Ruth Miska, Nancy Rothman, Susan Pollard, Ann & Skip Walker, Barbara & Ron Young, Kim Lally, Selma Abdo, Jeanette Roach, Sonja Knutsen, Greg & Heidi Ingram, Genny & Gerry Wilson, Barbara & Richard Jenkins, Barbara Berk, and James & Alice Heckman.

The friends who loaned me their tableware and treasures: Claudia Allin, Sarah Fairchild, Barbara Young, Cathy Obiedo, Lena Tabori, Amy Davis, John Kelly, Patty Westerbeke, Susy Pollard, Elli Fairchild, Kate Geddes, Linda Sunshine, Nancy Armstrong, Ruth Miska, Genny Wilson.

AND Jay Graham, my photographer, for his talent, sharp eye, incredible work ethic, and unflinching good temperament every single day we worked together.

—M.H.